Kumon English Reading & Writing

Grade 6

TABLE OF CONTENTS

Informational Writing 2

Narrative Writing.. 49

Argumentative Writing 102

Answer Key.. 141

KUMON

Kumon English Language Arts
Reading & Writing

INFORMATIONAL WRITING
Table of Contents

Activity	Title	Page
1:	Reading for Central Idea	4
2:	Writing a Summary	7
3:	Reading a Science Passage	10
4:	Writing an Introduction	13
5:	Reading for Structure	16
6:	Getting Started Writing an Informational Text	19
7:	Author's Purpose	22
8:	Research and Start Writing	25
9:	Discovering Confucius	28
10:	Looking at Language	31
11:	Making Connections	34
12:	Crafting an Introduction and a Conclusion	37
13:	Reviewing Author's Purpose	40
14:	Writing an Analysis	43
15:	Final Informational Piece	46

What do newspaper articles, nonfiction books, and documentaries all have in common? They are examples of informational texts. An informational text is simply a text that shares information. In fact, you could even describe the textbooks you use at school as informational texts! Without them, we wouldn't be able to learn about the world around us. In this section, you'll read five informational texts and analyze the way they present information. Then you'll use what you've learned to create a piece all of your own.

Activity 1: Reading for Central Idea

>> Read the passage below. If you see an unfamiliar word, circle it and look it up in a dictionary.

The Making of Books
By Helen Wieman Bledsoe

The books Confucius, one of the most well-known Chinese scholars, read were made of bamboo strips with words carved on their surfaces. The Chinese character for *book*, pronounced *ce*, is a picture of a bundle of long, narrow strips held together by a thin cord. To make these strips, bamboo shoots were cut in lengths and then dried over a fire. The outer green skin was cut off, leaving a smooth writing surface. It was only around A.D. 105, so tradition says, that paper was invented by a Chinese man named Cai Lun.

Scholars wrote with brushes that were made of bamboo or wood and tipped with ornamental tufts of rabbit, goat, or deer hair. Ink was made by mixing water with soot from a fire. To correct a mistake on bamboo, a writer needed only to scrape the error off with a special knife called a *xue*. Entire layers could be shaved off, and the strip used again.

These strips were stacked up or joined like an accordion and then tied together with a cord of silk, a fiber called hemp, or leather. The Chinese historian Sima Qian wrote that Confucius liked reading the Yi ("Book of Changes") so much that the "cords had been broken three times."

Wood was also used for books, especially official documents. Thin strips of poplar or willow were assembled in the same way as bamboo books. Wooden books, however, were sometimes rectangular in shape.

Silk fabric, a new invention of the Chinese in Confucius's day, was expensive and saved for very important books. Because it was lighter than bamboo, it was easier to carry. Silk that had not been dyed had a bright white color that made the brushstrokes stand out better than they did on bamboo or wood. Silk books were rolled up for storage.

Chinese writing, then as now, is done in columns of characters that start in the upper right-hand corner and run down the page and then across from right to left. Instead of an alphabet, their writing consists of pictographs, representing simplified pictures of an object, or ideographs, representing an idea such as justice or wisdom.

Books were handmade and, therefore, costly and rare. Before Confucius's time, only aristocrats had books in any quantity. Archaeologists have found some of these books in Chinese tombs. The court scribes responsible for the books held their offices by inheritance. Their descriptive family names are still the names of some modern-day Chinese families—Jian ("scribe"), Ji ("recorder"), and Shi ("historian").

Central idea: Informational texts give information about a topic. The central idea is the most important idea that the writer wants to explain. It is the reason the author writes the text. Sometimes the central idea is stated clearly in the opening of an informational text. Other times, you can figure it out by finding the most important details and using them to determine what is most important.

>> **Reread the passage. This time, underline important details as you read. Then answer the questions below:**

1. List four important details below:
   a. Ancient Chinese books were made of bamboo shoots.

   b. Scholars wrote with brushes and ink.

   c.

   d.

2. Think about what these details have in common. What is the biggest idea (or central idea) that the writer is telling us in this text?

   The central idea of this text is that in ancient China,

Reading for Central Idea

Text evidence: When you are speaking or writing about a text, you should always use evidence from the text to answer. Look back at the text and read what it says before answering. If you don't reread the text, you may misremember what it says or introduce your own ideas.

>> Use evidence from the text to answer the following questions:

3. How do we know that Confucius enjoyed reading the Book of Changes?
   a. The book was made of strips that were stacked like an accordion.
   b. The cords that bound the book were broken three times.
   c. He had the book bound in silk fabric.
   d. He often talked about reading it.

4. Why did only aristocrats own books?
   a. Other people weren't allowed to buy books.
   b. Silk was limited, so not many books could be made.
   c. Books were handmade, so they were expensive.
   d. Most people weren't interested in owning books.

5. Which of the following is NOT an advantage of silk books?
   a. They were lighter than bamboo.
   b. Brushstrokes showed more clearly than on bamboo.
   c. They could be rolled up for storage.
   d. They were very expensive to make.

6. List the characteristics of each type of book:

Bamboo	Wood	Silk

Writing a Summary

Summary: A summary retells the most important ideas in the text, without telling every single detail. A summary is shorter than the original text. It should not contain opinions about the text.

1. Which of the following things below are a summary? Write a checkmark if it is a summary. Write an x if it is not a summary, and then explain why in the line below.

    a. Your friend goes to see a movie. You ask them what the movie is about. They tell you everything that happened and even recite some of the dialogue for you.
    _____

    b. Your brother asks you about your favorite book. You tell him why you love it so much and what you think the best parts are.
    _____

    c. You ask your teacher to explain a news article to you. She gives a short, factual explanation of the most important parts of the article.
    _____

2. It can be helpful to organize your information before writing a summary. Use this space to record the central idea of "The Making of Books" and the most important details from each paragraph.

    Central Idea:

    Paragraph 1:

    Paragraph 2:

    Paragraph 3:

Paragraph 4:

Paragraph 5:

Paragraph 6:

Paragraph 7:

3. Use the details you recorded to write a summary of "The Making of Books." Make sure to keep your summary factual and to only include the most important details.

_____
_____
_____
_____
_____
_____
_____
_____
_____
_____
_____
_____
_____
_____

4. "The Making of Books" describes three different types of ancient Chinese books. Imagine you are creating your own type of book, different from the books we use today. What materials would you choose? What would the books look like? Describe your invention, and draw an illustration if you wish.

Writing a Summary

Activity 3: Reading a Science Passage

>> Read Part 1 of "Clues to the Past."

Clues to the Past: Part 1

By Lisa Gardiner

If you want to know the exact temperature outside, just look at a thermometer. If you want to know the average temperature in your region, you can check the recorded averages of many years in the area. But what if you want to know what the climate was like a few hundred or even a few thousand years ago? Since the development of the thermometer dates only to the 1600s, you will need to find another way. You will need to look for clues.

Amazing "Time Capsules"

Clues called "proxies" provide evidence of what climate was like hundreds to thousands of years ago. They are found in many different places—from tree trunks and coral skeletons to tiny bubbles in polar ice and layers of sand and mud. Some of these clues tell us what the temperature was like in the past. Others tell us how much rain and snow fell in an area.

To understand how ancient peoples lived in their environments, archaeologists look at proxies to understand what the climate was like at that time. For example, the Anasazi people living in the southwestern United States until about 700 years ago were affected by changes in the amount of rain. During times when water was plentiful, Anasazi communities grew. When there was drought, the communities shrank. It was by comparing clues to past climate with the findings from archaeological sites that scientists discovered this connection between the people and climate. While the story is more complicated because many factors affected the Anasazi, climate does seem to have played an important role.

How do proxies tell us about climate? Well, many proxies, including tree rings, corals, sediments, and ice, have layers that have formed over time. The thickness, color, and chemistry of the layers can be used to figure out what climate was like when the layer formed. Scientists often compare clues from a multitude of proxies, not just one, to figure out what climate was like. The examples that follow explain four different types of proxies that are used to determine what climate was like in the past.

1. Reread the passage. This time, as you read, underline key details. Then use those key details to determine the central idea, and write it below:

___

___

___

Determining the meaning of new vocabulary: When you read a text, pay close attention to any words that you are not familiar with. Use the following steps to determine the meaning of the word:

1. Read the sentence or sentences around the word, and look for clues. Sometimes the writer may use it with a synonym or another word with the same meaning. Other times, the writer may contrast the word with another word that has the opposite meaning.

2. Look for word parts that help you to guess the meaning of the word, like *un-*, *anti-*, or *dis-*.

3. Guess the meaning of the word based on the clues you've gathered. Then use a dictionary to confirm the meaning. Read each definition in the dictionary carefully. Some words have multiple definitions, and the best definition may not be the first one.

4. Reread the sentence(s) in the passage. You may want to try rephrasing the sentence in your own words to make sure it makes sense to you.

---

2. Find the first place in the passage where the word *proxies* is used. In this case, the author has included the definition of *proxies* for us. Write the part of the sentence that tells you the meaning of the word *proxies*:

___

___

___

3. Reread this sentence: "During times when water was plentiful, Anasazi communities grew. When there was *drought*, the communities shrank." Underline clues in the sentence that help you guess the meaning of the word *drought*. Then write your guess below.

___

___

___

Reading a Science Passage

4. Look up the word *drought* in a dictionary. Does it match your guess? Record the meaning in your own words:

_____

_____

5. Reread this sentence: "Scientists often compare clues from a *multitude* of proxies, not just one, to figure out what climate was like." Underline clues in the sentence that help you guess the meaning of the word *multitude*. Then write your guess below.

_____

_____

6. Look up the word *multitude* in a dictionary. Does it match your guess? Record the meaning in your own words:

_____

_____

7. Are there any other words in the passage that you are not familiar with? Record them and their meanings here.

Word	Meaning

Activity 4: Writing an Introduction

1. Reread Part 1 of "Clues to the Past." Use the space below to record the central idea and key details from each paragraph. Then use those details to write a short, objective summary of the passage.

   Central Idea:
   _____
   _____

   Paragraph 1:
   _____
   _____
   _____

   Paragraph 2:
   _____
   _____
   _____

   Paragraph 3:
   _____
   _____
   _____

   Paragraph 4:
   _____
   _____
   _____

   Summary:
   _____
   _____
   _____

Introductions

Think about how you would typically start a conversation with another person. What do you say first? Maybe you start with "Hi, how are you?" If you haven't met the person before, then you probably share your name and some information about yourself. If you just started talking to them about something serious without saying "hello" first, they would probably be a little confused!

Just as in a conversation, texts usually start with an introduction. In an informational text, the introduction can serve several purposes:

- To introduce the central idea
- To get the reader's attention and interest them in reading more
- To explain to the reader what the text will be about

2. Reread the introduction to "Clues to the Past."

   If you want to know the exact temperature outside, just look at a thermometer. If you want to know the average temperature in your region, you can check the recorded averages of many years in the area. But what if you want to know what the climate was like a few hundred or even a few thousand years ago? Since the development of the thermometer dates only to the 1600s, you will need to find another way. You will need to look for clues.

3. Whom is the writer talking to in this introduction? What effect did that have on you as you read?

   _____

   _____

   _____

4. One technique writers sometimes use is to describe an everyday experience that the reader will be familiar with. Then they use it as a way to explain something the reader might not know about. What everyday experience does Lisa Gardiner describe in the introduction to "Clues to the Past"? What is the unfamiliar experience she describes?

   _____

   _____

   _____

   _____

5. Imagine you are writing an informational text about the weather in your hometown. Write an introduction that gets the readers' attention and communicates the central idea, or what the whole text will be about.

Activity 5: Reading for Structure

>> Read the text below. As you read, circle any unfamiliar words.

Clues to the Past: Part 2
By Lisa Gardiner

What Trees Say

Each year, tree trunks grow a little wider—adding a layer of new wood just inside of the bark. This layer is called a tree ring. When climate is warm, the growing season is longer, and trees grow very thick rings. In some areas of the world, trees grow thick rings during years when there is lots of rain.

How do you look at a living tree's rings without cutting it down? Scientists use a tool called a borer to extract a small cylinder of wood called a core from the tree. The core is about as thick as a drinking straw but is much longer if it is from an old tree.

What Corals Say

Each year, corals living in tropical seas add layers to their rocky skeletons. The thickness of the layers depends on water temperature, the depth where it is living in the ocean, and the amount of cloud cover in the sky above the ocean. The chemistry of the layers is also evidence of past climate. For instance, the types of oxygen that are in the layers depend on the temperature of the seawater where the coral lived.

Since corals can live for many thousands of years, they offer a good record of how the temperature of seawater changed through time. To get to the clues trapped in a coral's skeleton, scuba-diving scientists drill into the coral with a special underwater drill and extract a core.

What Ice Says

You might expect that the ice sheets covering most of Greenland and Antarctica are evidence of cold climate. But the ice contains evidence of what climate was like worldwide, not just where the ice formed.

Ice sheets form in layers over time. The one at the top formed recently from snow that fell on the ice sheet. Those at the bottom formed hundreds of thousands of years ago. An analysis of the different layers offers clues as to what climate was like at specific times in the past. Scientists also look at dust and volcanic ash preserved within the ice to learn more about past climate.

Bubbles of air trapped in the ice provide a snapshot of what the atmosphere was like when the bubble formed. Bubbles of ancient air are analyzed to figure out how much greenhouse gas used to be in the air. Because greenhouse gas traps heat, the amount in air bubbles is a clue to temperature readings in the past.

What Lakes Say

Some scientists look for clues about past climates deep in the sand and mud at the bottom of lakes. Within those layers of sediment are grains of pollen. Plants release pollen into the air, and some of the pollen falls on lakes, sinking to the bottom, where it is preserved in the sediments.

The pollen within the sediments can help scientists identify which plants used to live near the lake. Some plants prefer warm temperatures, while others prefer cold temperatures. Likewise, some plants require a large amount of water, while others need much less. By figuring out how the plants that lived near the lake changed over time, scientists can chart how climate changed near the lake.

Editor's note: Since the barometer and thermometer were invented in the 1600s, to determine climate in earlier periods, scientists infer the climate record from physical and biological fossil data. This data includes oxygen isotope ratios detected in ice cores, tree-ring dating, archaeological discoveries, and ice floe and glacier data. Records intended for other purposes, such as weather diaries, shipping logs, tax records, crop production, and pricing records, also act as reference material.

1. Record the unfamiliar words you circled in the chart below. Use context clues to guess the meaning of the word, and then verify its definition using a dictionary.

Word	Definition

2. Look back at the text. Underline each of the section headings ("What _____ Say(s)).

3. Use the space below to summarize each of the sections:

What Trees Say:

_____

_____

Reading for Structure

What Corals Say:
_____
_____

What Ice Says:
_____
_____

What Lakes Say:
_____
_____

4. Why do you think the author included these headings? How would the text be different if it didn't have these headings?
_____
_____
_____

5. Now reread the editor's note. Why do you think the editor included this note? Is this information useful to the reader? Why or why not?
_____
_____

6. When you are reading a long informational text, it can be helpful to look at the organizational structure. Here is an outline of "Clues from the Past."
   - Introduction: tells the reader what the text is about
   - Amazing "Time Capsules": explains how scientists look for different types of clues
   - What Trees Say: tells how scientists can use trees to study the past
   - What Corals Say: tells how scientists can use coral to study the past
   - What Ice Says: tells how scientists can use ice to study the past
   - What Lakes Say: tells how scientists can use lakes to study the past
   - Editor's note: gives an extra piece of information

   Look back at Part 1, and reread "Amazing 'Time Capsules.'" Find the sentences that explain how the rest of the text will be organized. Record them here:
   _____
   _____
   _____

Activity 6: Getting Started Writing an Informational Text

1. In Activity 15, you will write an informational text of your own. In this activity, you will choose your topic and create a plan. Your topic should be something that interests you and that you already know a bit about. If you need to do some research, that's OK too. Here are some ideas to get you started:

   - Favorite animal
   - Favorite sport
   - A city or place that interests me
   - A hobby or interest that I know a lot about
   - A person I admire

   Choose one of these ideas, and do a freewrite below to choose your topic.

   _____
   _____
   _____
   _____
   _____
   _____

2. Now that you have chosen your topic, it's time to brainstorm what you want to say about the topic. For example, if you are writing about an animal, you might want to include information about its habitat, appearance, life cycle, and diet. Use the chart below to organize your ideas.

Topic:	
1.	2.
3.	4.

3. Look back at the outline for "Clues from the Past" in Activity 5. Draft an outline for your piece below. You should include an introduction, a conclusion, and the things about your topic that you brainstormed above.

_____
_____
_____
_____
_____
_____
_____
_____
_____
_____
_____
_____
_____
_____
_____
_____
_____

4. What questions do you have about your topic that you will need to answer before you write your piece? Write your questions below.

_____
_____
_____
_____
_____

5. Use this space to draft your introduction. Your introduction should get the reader interested in the topic and explain to them what the text will be about.

Activity 7: Author's Purpose

>> Read the text below. Circle any unfamiliar words.

The Horse: Wild and Free
by Pat Betteley

The horse has been friend and helper to humans since Asian nomads tamed horses 5,500 years ago. For centuries, people depended on horses for transportation, farming, and hunting. Horses and their riders also were honored for their heroism in battle. But did you know that this domesticated animal originally roamed Earth as a wild animal? And that the first horses were closer in size to a modern-day large dog? North America's wild horses actually are feral horses, descendants of domesticated horses.

For a horse to be truly wild, it would have to have no ancestors that were domesticated. The Przewalski's horse is believed by some to be the only still-living example of a wild horse. Known to the Mongols as takhis, these sturdy horses once lived freely in the Eurasian Steppes. Przewalski's horses were last seen in the wild in Mongolia in 1968. Today, they are mainly found in zoos and nature preserves, though there have been some efforts to reintroduce them to the wild. What we think of as wild horses are actually feral horses. Feral horses are descended from horses that were once domesticated but that have run free for generations. They either escaped from domesticity or were set free. The Australian brumby is a feral horse that was introduced by English settlers hundreds of years ago.

Free-Roaming Horses

Perhaps the most famous feral horses are the free-roaming herds of mustangs in North America. They are descendants of European horses brought to the Americas more than 500 years ago. In a strange twist of fate, scientists believe that today's mustangs also are descended from North America's original horses. Thousands of years ago, those horses traveled northward in the Americas and over the Bering Strait land bridge between Alaska and Russia's Siberia. They spread throughout Asia and Europe. Meanwhile, horses became extinct in the Americas, most likely due to climate change and overhunting.

Then, in the 1490s, the Spanish conquistadors reintroduced horses to the Americas. Some Indigenous peoples acquired and bred the horses in the wild. Known as mestengos (stray animals), the horses were fast and difficult to catch and train. In the end, many of the creatures were left to run wild.

By the mid-1800s, an estimated two million mustangs, which is the English term for mestengos, lived in North America. That number dropped to about 17,000 a century later. Considered a nuisance by ranchers in the West, mustangs were captured and killed. In 1971, a federal law was passed to protect mustangs on public land. The Wild Free-Roaming Horses and Burros Act identified the animals as important symbols of the "pioneer spirit of the West." Today, there are about 88,000 free-roaming horses in the western United States.

1. Record the unfamiliar words you circled in the chart below. Use context clues to guess the meaning of the word, and then verify its definition using a dictionary.

Word	Definition

2. Reread the text, and then write a summary.

___

> The author's purpose is the reason the writer writes their text. In an informational text, the purpose is usually to inform the reader about something specific. You can usually figure out the author's purpose by reading the introduction and by paying attention to the facts and examples in the informational text.

Author's Purpose

3. What is the author's purpose in writing this text?

   a. To tell about the Spanish conquistadors

   b. To explain the history of wild horses in America

   c. To explain the difference between domesticated horses and wild horses

   d. To tell about why there are so few mustangs left

4. Return back to "The Horse: Wild and Free." Underline the sentences that helped you find the author's purpose.

5. In the space below, write a paragraph explaining how the author used facts and examples to achieve their purpose for writing.

Activity 8: Research and Start Writing

1. You just read the text "The Horse: Wild and Free," which contains many facts about wild horses and how they came to be in the United States. In this activity, you will gather the facts you need for your own informational text. Review the questions you wrote in Activity 6. If you have any additional questions to answer, write them here.

   _____
   _____
   _____
   _____
   _____
   _____
   _____
   _____

2. Ask an adult to help you search for the answers online. Use this space below to record what you learn.

   _____
   _____
   _____
   _____
   _____
   _____
   _____
   _____
   _____
   _____
   _____

3. Look back at the outline you drafted in Activity 6. Choose one body paragraph (not the introduction or conclusion) to draft in this space. Use some of the facts you learned through your research, as well as what you already know. Remember that you do not need to include every fact. Only use facts that are interesting and relevant to the topic you are explaining.

4. How did the writing process go for you? What did you find difficult? What did you find easy? What will you need to work on before you write your final piece?

Activity 9: Discovering Confucius

>> Read the text below. Circle any unfamiliar words.

Discovering Confucius: Part 1

by Gloria W. Lannom

Commander He Shuliang was facing the worst problem that could confront a Chinese man. A military hero and government official of the Zhou dynasty, he lacked a healthy son to carry on the family line and inherit his property. His first wife had given birth to nine daughters, while his second had given birth to a boy who was unable to work due to his health.

At age 70, Commander He was running out of time. He arranged a third marriage, and in 551 B.C., his third wife bore him the male heir he desired. This boy grew up to be the renowned sage Confucius. Confucius was born in a small village near Qufu, the capital of the State of Lu, in present-day Shandong Province. With his big head and big nose, he was not considered an attractive child, but he was healthy and strong, and that was what mattered to his father. Confucius grew very tall, over six feet. Later writings said his height was nine feet, but most likely his followers used this exaggeration to highlight that he was exceptional.

Death Changes All

Confucius was three when He Shuliang died. Officials then judged his parents' union to be illegal. There was a great age difference between his parents, and the other wives and relatives were not about to admit Confucius into the family circle. As a result, mother and son were left penniless. For years, Confucius worked at raising livestock, recordkeeping, and other low-level jobs. Later, he did become minister of crime, but he never forgot what it was like to do hard labor and live a life of poverty. Perhaps this explains why he accepted men of humble birth as his disciples, or followers.

Confucius and his mother were very close. When she died, he wanted to bury her near his father but did not know the site of the grave. When he finally discovered it, he was able to fulfill the proper duty a son owed a parent. Tradition says that, as a small child, Confucius had enjoyed arranging ritual objects on the family altar, a pastime that perhaps led to his later respect for the behavior and traditional values practiced during the early Zhou dynasty.

A Time To Study

By age 15, Confucius had developed a deep love of learning. In China at that time, tutors taught youths of noble birth, but Confucius's inferior economic and social circumstances prevented him from joining such a group. Most likely, he attended a local school, and although the names of the masters who taught him are known, in later life he never called anyone his permanent teacher.

Confucius undertook an extensive self-study of the classics, including the *Book of Odes* (*Shijing* in Chinese), for he loved poetry. Confucius probably read the books at the government offices in Qufu because he would not have owned personal copies. At the time, paper had not been invented, so books were written on bamboo strips attached with leather thongs and bound into heavy volumes.

1. Record the unfamiliar words you circled in the chart below. Use context clues to guess the meaning of the word, and then verify its definition using a dictionary.

Word	Definition

2. Which of the following best describes a young Confucius?

    a. He was a wealthy heir to a large family.

    b. He was nine feet tall.

    c. He grew up poor and had to work hard.

    d. He had a poor relationship with his mother.

3. Confucianism teaches that children have a responsibility to honor their parents and older family members. What details from the text explain why Confucius may have held those beliefs? Reread paragraphs 3 and 4, and then write the details below.

___

___

___

___

___

Discovering Confucius

4. Confucius had a love of learning, even though it was difficult for him to get an education. What evidence does the author include to show Confucius's love of learning? Record the evidence below.

_____

_____

_____

_____

_____

_____

5. In Activity 1, you read "The Making of Books," which tells about how books were made during the time of Confucius. Look back at "The Making of Books." How does this text help you understand more about Confucius's passion for studying. You can use these sentence frames in your response:

In Confucius's time, books were made of _____.

When Confucius was alive, only _____ could own books.

Although Confucius was poor, _____.

_____

_____

_____

_____

_____

_____

_____

_____

_____

_____

_____

_____

_____

_____

_____

Activity 10: Looking at Language

Writers often use transition words to show relationships between ideas. Look at the italic words below.

"Officials then judged his parents' union to be illegal. . . . *As a result*, mother and son were left penniless."

As a result shows cause and effect. Confucius and his mother were left penniless because his parents' union was found to be illegal.

"*Later*, he did become minister of crime, but he never forgot what it was like to do hard labor and live a life of poverty."

Later helps us understand when the action took place—some time after his experiences as a child.

"*At the time*, paper had not been invented, so books were written on bamboo strips attached with leather thongs and bound into heavy volumes."

At the time lets us know that we are talking about a specific time period—in this case, the time Confucius was alive.

Here are some common transitions:

Cause/effect: As a result, so, because, due to

Time: Later, at the time, then, meanwhile

1. Look back at Activity 7. Find as many transitions as possible. Write them here.

___
___
___
___
___
___
___
___
___

2. Now look back at the writing you have already drafted. Are there any places where you can add transitions? Rewrite the new sentences below.

3. Confucius had a difficult childhood. Write a diary entry from the point of view of Confucius as a child. What might he have been doing, thinking, and feeling? Use at least two transitions in your writing.

Activity 11 — Making Connections

>> Read the text below. Circle any unfamiliar words.

Discovering Confucius: Part 2
by Gloria W. Lannom

Time for Change

In the sixth century B.C., the State of Lu was in decline. Sandwiched between larger states competing for power, it endured multiple invasions, and government officials conducted business in an environment of bribery and corruption.

Confucius was dismayed by the behavior of officials who had been appointed because of their family's standing and not their ability. In what is known as the Five Classics, he found what he believed was the ideal way to rule—a way that had been standard under the founder of the Zhou dynasty. Confucius believed that moral government could be restored if the rituals, correct behavior, honesty, and other principles of that past "golden age" were followed. Therefore, he made it his mission to search for a ruler who would follow these ideals.

The Transmitter

Although Confucius married early and had several children, he spent little time with his family. Instead, he devoted himself to his disciples, instructing them through his explanations of the Five Classics. Confucius never wanted to be called "teacher." Rather, he preferred to be known as a transmitter, declaring, "I transmit but do not create."

Confucius strictly observed the rules of correct behavior, but sometimes he could be short-tempered, particularly when his students failed to understand his message. He never wrote an autobiography, and no one wrote his biography during his lifetime. The *Analects*—that is, the sayings of Confucius—was compiled after his death. Another primary source that includes information about Confucius is *The Zuo Commentary*. This official government record includes information on the culture of the times and mentions Confucius's travels and death.

Biographic details also appear in *Records of the Historian* by Sima Qian, the renowned chronicler of the Han dynasty. Writing more than 400 years after Confucius lived, Sima Qian questioned whether some of the facts he reported were entirely accurate.

There are also many legends about Confucius. Unfortunately, these delightful tales of superhuman abilities do little to reveal the "real" Confucius. They do, however, offer proof of how the Confucius's disciples and admirers inflated his reputation as one way of showing their respect for him.

1. Record the unfamiliar words you circled in the chart below. Use context clues to guess the meaning of the word, and then verify its definition using a dictionary.

Word	Definition

2. In paragraph 2, Gloria W. Lannom writes, "Confucius was dismayed by the behavior of officials who had been appointed because of their family's standing and not their ability." What parts of Confucius's own experiences might have led him to feel this way? Why do you think he emphasized choosing officials based on ability rather than family connections? Be sure to cite details from the text, including Part 1.

_____
_____
_____
_____
_____
_____
_____
_____

Making Connections

3. In Activity 1, you read "The Making of Books," which is an informational text about books in ancient China. In Activities 9 and 11, you read "Discovering Confucius," a biography of Confucius. How are these texts similar? How are they different? Fill out the chart below.

Things you notice about "The Making of Books"	Things you notice about both texts	Things you notice about "Discovering Confucius"

4. Why do you think it is important to read both types of informational texts? What understandings can you gain from reading both texts together?

_____
_____
_____
_____
_____
_____
_____

Activity 12: Crafting an Introduction and a Conclusion

1. Reread the introduction to "Discovering Confucius." Remember that a strong introduction grabs the reader's attention and also tells them what the rest of the piece will be about. What do you notice about this introduction? Do you feel that this introduction accomplishes these two things? Use evidence to support your opinion.

   _____
   _____
   _____
   _____
   _____
   _____
   _____
   _____
   _____

2. Reread the conclusion to "Discovering Confucius." Remember that a strong conclusion wraps up the piece and gives the reader a sense of closure. What do you notice about this conclusion? Do you feel that this conclusion accomplishes these two things? Use evidence to support your opinion.

   _____
   _____
   _____
   _____
   _____
   _____
   _____
   _____
   _____

3. Use this space to try writing an introduction to your piece again. You can take the one you already drafted in Activity 6 and revise it, or you can start with a fresh draft. Think about the things that worked well in the example you just read, and try to use them in your own writing.

_____
_____
_____
_____
_____
_____
_____
_____
_____
_____

4. Use this space to draft a conclusion to your opinion piece. Think about what worked well in the example you just read, and try to do the same thing in your own conclusion.

_____
_____
_____
_____
_____
_____
_____
_____
_____
_____

5. Just for fun: Imagine you are Confucius. Write a diary entry about why you love to read.

Activity 13: Reviewing Author's Purpose

>> Read the text below. Circle any unfamiliar words.

The Nose Knows

By Barbara Gowan

Did you know that a dog can have more than 220 million sensory cells in its nose, while humans have only 5 million? Dogs have INCREDIBLE noses!

"Find it!" commands the handler. Tucker, a black Lab, crouches on the bow of the research boat and sniffs the ocean air. The captain turns the boat in the direction Tucker's black nose is pointing. This dog can smell the scent of killer whale, or orca, excrement (called "scat") from more than a mile away.

Biologists examine the scat to learn why the orca population is declining in Washington's Puget Sound.

Super-snooper canines also help scientists in other ways. Some locate underground fungus that is killing pine trees, for example. And in Florida's Everglades National Park, the beagle Python Pete has used his nose to find exotic pythons preying on wildlife.

A dog's keen sense of smell helps humans in many ways. A change in body odor of a person with diabetes can trigger a medical alert dog to bark to warn its owner that their blood sugar is dangerously low. Service dogs protect kids who have peanut allergies by sniffing an area and blocking a child from entering if there is a danger. Trained dogs also can distinguish between breath samples of healthy people and patients with cancer. Scientists hope that man's best friend can become a new tool in cancer screening.

Four-legged law enforcers protect our country. The Beagle Brigade inspects baggage at international airports. It's a game of hide-and-seek as the hounds search for prohibited fruits, meats, and plants that could be carrying harmful pests and diseases. German shepherds and Belgian Malinois work with border-patrol agents as drug-sniffing specialists. They've discovered illegal substances in tires, in gas tanks, and even inside a car's engine. Our subways, trains, and crowded city streets are safer because of the work of dogs who are trained to detect the moving scent of explosives.

All dogs have an amazing ability to collect scents and separate the parts of the odor. A person would smell chili cooking, but a dog can smell the meat, the beans, the tomatoes, and each seasoning. From a single drop of urine, a sniffing dog learns what animal it came from, its diet, its health, and whether it's a friend or an enemy.

So if you have a pet dog, watch it sniff. After all, a dog's nose knows!

1. Record the unfamiliar words you circled in the chart below. Use context clues to guess the meaning of the word, and then verify its definition using a dictionary.

Word	Definition

2. Write a summary of "The Nose Knows."

_____

_____

_____

_____

_____

3. What is the author's purpose in writing this text?

   a. To explain why German shepherds are used in airports

   b. To explain how good dogs are at smelling things

   c. To explain how service dogs do their jobs

   d. To explain how dogs help do research

Reviewing Author's Purpose   41

4. What details does Barbara Gowan include to help achieve this purpose? List four.
   -
   -
   -
   -

5. Reread paragraph 5. Why do you think the writer included this paragraph? How does this paragraph help the writer achieve her purpose?

   _____
   _____
   _____
   _____
   _____
   _____
   _____
   _____

Activity 14: Writing an Analysis

1. In this activity, you will write an analysis of "The Nose Knows." First reread the text. Write an informal reaction below. How do you feel after reading this text? What did you learn? What questions did you have? Did you enjoy reading this text? Why or why not?

_____

Writing an Analysis 43

2. An informational text should explain a topic clearly to the reader using facts, details, and examples that are well-organized and easy to follow. It should have an introduction that gets the reader's attention and explains what the text will be about. It should also have a conclusion that wraps up the piece. Take notes below on each element of "The Nose Knows."

Introduction	
Conclusion	
Facts, Details, Examples	
Organization	

3. Now answer the following: How did Barbara Gowan develop her topic in this informational piece? Did she successfully explain this topic? Do you have any critiques of her piece?

_____
_____
_____
_____
_____
_____
_____
_____
_____
_____
_____
_____
_____
_____
_____
_____

4. What aspects of this text do you want to use in your own writing? What do you want to avoid?

_____
_____
_____
_____
_____

Activity 15: Final Informational Piece

>> **In this activity, you will write your informational text. Use this page to create your outline. Then use the next two pages to write your text.**

Be sure that your informational text:

- Focuses on a clear topic
- Introduces the topic to the reader in an engaging way
- Has organized ideas that are easy to follow
- Contains facts and examples about the topic
- Ends in a clear way

Kumon English Language Arts
Reading & Writing

NARRATIVE WRITING
Table of Contents

Activity	Title	Page
16:	Making Inferences	51
17:	Structuring a Story	54
18:	Sensory Language	57
19:	Establishing Setting and Characters	60
20:	Analyzing Conflict	63
21:	Writing about Conflict	66
22:	Conflict Resolution	69
23:	Bringing It Home	72
24:	Diving into Fantasy	75
25:	Building Character	78
26:	Understanding Character	81
27:	Dialogue	84
28:	Plotting It Out	87
29:	Organizing Events	90
30:	Reading Biography	93
31:	Using Signal Words	96
32:	Final Narrative Piece	99

We've all seen the power of a good piece of narrative writing, whether it's a bedtime story, an exciting book, or a thrilling TV show. Sometimes the characters are just like us. Other times they have magic powers or rocket ships with laser beams! Stories can be funny, scary, or sad—and they can also be true. In this section, you'll analyze four very different pieces of narrative writing. Then you'll use what you know to begin drafting a story all your own. Get ready to be creative!

Activity 16: Making Inferences

>> Read the story below.

The Gift

by Roderick J. Robinson

As he lay awake one night, Bebeto could hear his parents discussing his sister Ana's birthday. It was just two days away. Birthdays were always a lot of fun, even though they did not have store-bought gifts. Nearly all of the toys he and his sister had were homemade. There was nothing wrong with that, he knew. Many families in his neighborhood were poor.

This birthday would be different, though. Ana was older now, and he'd seen how her eyes lit up when she saw the new doll at Zulma's Presentes, a neighborhood store near their house.

How he longed for her to have it! An idea finally came to him just before he drifted off to sleep. After a quick breakfast the following morning, he placed a tin can and a piece of string in a burlap sack. Then he tied the sack to the handlebars of his bicycle and headed toward the outskirts of town.

The road grew steeper as he neared the outskirts of the town, and when he reached the hill country, he had to get off and push the bike the rest of the way. After a long trek, he reached his destination, the mango grove.

There were already two other boys there, standing among some smaller trees and picking fruit from the lower branches. Bebeto grabbed his sack and set to work right away. The smaller trees had already been picked over, but he was able to find a half dozen mangoes before noon. When the sun was high overhead, the hard work began. Nearly all of the taller trees held ripe mangoes, but they were well beyond reach.

The other boys took their fruit and went away. Bebeto said goodbye. Then he cut down a long piece of bamboo growing at the edge of the grove. He took the tin can from the sack, tied it to one end of the bamboo stick, and walked over to the base of a mature mango tree.

He stayed there, poking the tin can high up into the tree. His efforts were occasionally rewarded when a reddish-green mango plunked into the can. After a while his neck ached from looking upward, and his arms grew sore. He kept at it, though, and by late afternoon his sack was nearly full.

On the way back to town, Bebeto began to worry that the other boys might already have sold or traded their mangoes to Zulma. Maybe he was too late. But he reached her store just as she was closing—in time to exchange some of his mangoes for the doll.

The following morning, Ana walked into the kitchen and took a seat at the breakfast table.

"Good morning, birthday girl," said her mother, pouring her a glass of passion fruit juice and handing her a piece of sweet bread with lemon jelly on top. "I hear your brother has a special surprise for you today."

Just then Bebeto came in, carrying a large bowl of mangoes. He placed it on the table before Ana.

"Happy birthday, Sis," he said.

"My favorite fruit—thank you, Bebeto!" said Ana.

She reached for the bowl and picked up the top mango. Then her eyes widened, and her smile beamed even brighter. There, nestled among the fruit, was the new doll.

1. You can use text evidence to answer questions about a narrative text, just as you would for an informational passage. Use text evidence to answer: How was Bebeto able to get enough mangoes to trade for the doll?

    a. He took them from the shorter mango trees.

    b. The other boys gave him their mangoes.

    c. He used a tin can to collect mangoes from up high.

    d. He climbed the tree to pick them with his hands.

2. What text evidence best supports your answer to question 1?

    a. "The other boys took their fruit and went away. Bebeto said goodbye."

    b. "He stayed there, poking the tin can high up into the tree. His efforts were occasionally rewarded when a reddish-green mango plunked into the can."

    c. "On the way back to town, Bebeto began to worry that the other boys might already have sold or traded their mangoes to Zulma. Maybe he was too late."

    d. "The road grew steeper as he neared the outskirts of the town, and when he reached the hill country, he had to get off and push the bike the rest of the way."

> You can use details in the story to help answer text evidence questions. You can also use them to draw inferences. An inference is something that is not directly stated in the story. In order to draw an inference, you have to hunt for clues.

3. Reread paragraph 1. Why does Bebeto's family not exchange store-bought presents? Underline the clues that help explain. Then write your inference below.

_____

_____

_____

4. Roderick J. Robinson doesn't directly tell us what Bebeto is like, but through his actions we can draw inferences about him as a character. How do you think Bebeto feels about his sister? What evidence can you find to support this inference? You can use these sentence frames to get started: Bebeto wants his sister to _____ because _____. I know this because _____.

_____

_____

_____

_____

> Narrative texts have themes. A theme is a statement that summarizes the point of the story. It is like a central idea or sometimes a lesson that is learned. For example, one example of a theme is: Make new friends, but keep the old.

5. Like informational texts, narrative texts can also have a central idea, which is also called a theme. Which of the following is the best choice for the theme?

   a. Teamwork can make a task easier.

   b. Money can solve any problem.

   c. Be loyal to your friends.

   d. The best gift of all is love from your family.

6. Go back to the text, and find evidence to support the theme you chose. On the lines below, explain how the evidence helped you choose this theme.

_____

_____

_____

_____

Making Inferences 53

Activity 17: Structuring a Story

Most stories contain the follow parts: a beginning, a middle, and an end. In the beginning, the characters are introduced, and the setting is described. Sometimes a conflict, or problem, is also introduced. In the middle, the characters face the main conflict, and there are events that happen. In the end, there is a resolution, or an ending to the conflict. Hopefully, the problem is solved! In some stories, the problem may not be fully solved, but the characters learn and grow.

Understanding how narratives are told is helpful for understanding a narrative text because it allows you to break up the text as you read it and understand each part. It will also help you to create your own.

1. Fill out the table below to organize what you know about "The Gift."

Characters: who is in the story?	
Beginning: what happens first?	
Middle: what happens in the middle?	
End: what happens last?	

2. Use the details you wrote above to write a short summary of "The Gift." Remember that summaries contain only the most important details. Summaries should be shorter than the original text. They should also be objective, or factual. They should not contain your opinion.

_____

_____

_____

3. In Activity 32, you will write your own narrative. Remember that narratives can be fiction, like a story. They can also be nonfiction, like a biography or memoir. You can write about any topic you wish, but here are some ideas to get started:

   - Write a story about an astronaut going into space. How do they feel about the trip? What happens to them in space? What problems might they face, and how will they solve them?

   - Write a sequel to your favorite book, movie, or TV show. Are there any new characters you'd like to add? Where will it take place? What new problems will the characters face?

   - Think about an interesting thing that happened recently to you or someone you know. How can you turn it into a story? Can you give it a beginning, middle, and end? Who are the characters, and where does it take place?

   Choose one of these topics or a topic of your own. Write your topic here.

4. Use this space to do a freewrite about your topic. You will have lots of time in the upcoming activities to draft your story. This is a space to write informally about what interests you about this topic and to brainstorm any ideas that pop into your head. Your goal should not be perfect writing—it's OK to write down an idea that might not make it into the final story. Instead, try to keep your pen or pencil moving and the ideas flowing. Remember: there are no bad ideas when you are starting to brainstorm!

Activity 18: Sensory Language

>> Read the story below.

My Grandma Talley (Part 1)
by Nadine Oduor

At Grandma Talley's feet, watching her sip iced tea and wave at passing cars.

"Whew! This weather's right sultry," she complained, her rocking chair creaking back and forth on her front porch. Her flowered cotton dress stuck to her back, damp with sweat. She took a swig of tea from her cold glass. "Go ahead on, Kincaid. Pour yourself another glass," she urged.

Ice cubes clinked against crystal as I picked up the frosty pitcher of tea and poured some into my glass.

It was a muggy day in Wink, Texas, with the lemon yellow sun rising high in the noonday sky. The breeze from the hand fan, given to Grandma Talley by Reverend Fontaine of Sweet Home Baptist Church, blew back her floppy straw hat, making it flap like silk butterfly wings. She fanned her wrinkled mahogany face with one gnarled hand and waved at people passing by with the other.

I smiled, my mouth tasting bitter and sweet from the lemons and sugar.

"See my pink rosebush growin' up the north side of my fence, Kincaid?" Grandma Talley asked.

"Yes, ma'am, I do," I answered.

"And see that little bush between the jack-in-the-pulpits and mountain laurel?" she asked.

"Yes, ma'am, I do," I answered again. The humidity was making me awful tired and sleepy. I thought about going home and taking a nap, but it was the middle of the day and I had chores to do. I gulped down the tea, then placed the empty glass on the porch floorboards, mindful of the gaping spaces between them.

"That little rosebush flourishes almost anywhere, sending roots down deep, searching for nourishment, for life," Grandma Talley continued. "Roses take a lotta tender lovin' care, they do. Gotta know just how much water to give 'em and when. The blossoms turned out beautiful and strong. Kinda' remind me of you, Kincaid."

"Thanks." I blushed and busily braided one of my plaits that had come undone.

"Hi ya'll doing, Miz Grissom?" Grandma Talley shouted, waving to a woman passing by in a beat-up Ford pickup truck that slowed to a snail's pace in front of the house.

"Pretty fine," Miz Grissom answered. "And you?"

Miz Grissom's car went on down the street after Grandma Talley grunted, "Mighty fine myself!"

My kitten, Miz Moonlight, slinked around the corner of the house and crawled into my lap. I stroked her gleaming silver white coat, soft as cotton candy against my hand.

"That cat near 'bout scared me outta my wits," Grandma Talley laughed.

"She's quiet as a ghost, most times," I admitted.

"I bet she'd have a whole lotta stories to tell, if only the cat didn't have her tongue." Grandma Talley cackled.

I thought that was pretty funny and giggled. Grandma Talley's deep molasses laugh made her stomach jiggle, and I imagined her laughter bubbling up inside her heart to her throat, then sashaying out her caramel-colored lips.

Characters are the people (or sometimes animals, dragons, etc.) that the story is about. The setting is where and when a story takes place. When you begin a story, pay attention to the characters and setting and how the author describes them. They are important story elements.

Sometimes, the story may be told by one of the characters, called the narrator. In this story, Kincaid is the narrator. You can tell because she uses words like *I* when telling the story.

1. List the characters in Part 1 of "My Grandma Talley."

   _____
   _____
   _____

2. Where does "My Grandma Talley" take place?

   _____
   _____
   _____

3. Part 1 of "My Grandma Talley" contains many details about Grandma Talley and the narrator, Kincaid. List some details here. Then see if you can draw some inferences about these characters.

Character	Details	Inferences
Grandma Talley	"She fanned her <u>wrinkled mahogany face</u> with one <u>gnarled hand</u> and waved at people passing by with the other."	Grandma Talley is old.
	"'Hi ya'll doing, Miz Grissom?' Grandma Talley shouted, waving to a woman passing by in a beat-up Ford pickup truck that slowed to a snail's pace in front of the house."	
Kincaid	"I thought about going home and taking a nap, but it was the middle of the day and I had chores to do."	Kincaid is responsible.
	"'Thanks.' I <u>blushed</u> and busily braided one of my plaits that had come undone."	

> Sensory details are details that appeal to one of the five senses: smell, taste, touch, sight, and hearing.

4. Nadine Oduor uses many sensory details to describe the setting. Find as many as you can, and list them below.

Sight	"her gleaming silver white coat"
Touch	"Her flowered cotton dress stuck to her back, damp with sweat."
Hearing	
Taste	

Sensory Language 59

Activity 19: Establishing Setting and Characters

1. What is the setting for your story? Include the place and the time period.

   _____
   _____
   _____
   _____

2. As you saw in Part 1 of "My Grandma Talley," sensory details help make a setting come to life. Write some sensory details about the setting for your story. Try writing at least two for each sense. You don't have to include all of these in your final story, but it's good to brainstorm as many as possible when you're getting started.

Sight		
Smell		
Taste		
Touch		
Hearing		

3. Now list the characters in your story here.

   _____
   _____
   _____

4. Use this space to brainstorm details about three characters from your story. If your story has more than three characters, choose the most important characters.

	Character 1: _____	**Character 2:** _____	**Character 3:** _____
How they look			
What their personality is like			
What they want in this story			

> Some stories are told in the third person. When a story is told in the third person, the characters are all described using pronouns like *he, she, they,* and *them*. When a story is told in the first person, there is a narrator telling the story to the reader. They use pronouns like *I, me,* and *my.* Kincaid is the narrator of "My Grandma Talley." We know this because of sentences like this: "Ice cubes clinked against crystal as I picked up the frosty pitcher of tea and poured some into my glass."
>
> The advantage of using a first-person narrator is that the reader can get closer to the person telling the story. The advantage of telling a story in the third person is that the reader gets to hear about each character without judgment.

Establishing Setting and Characters

5. Will you tell this story in the third person or first person? If you tell it in the first person, who will the narrator be? Use this space to do a freewrite to determine the benefits of each possibility.

Activity 20: Analyzing Conflict

>> Read Part 2 of the story below. Circle any unfamiliar words.

My Grandma Talley (Part 2)
by Nadine Oduor

"Everybody and everything's got a life story," Grandma Talley began but was suddenly interrupted by an annoying fly buzzing around her head. "Child, hand me that swatter over there."

I gave it to her, and she hit at the pesky insect, missing by a gossamer wing. The fly zigzagged into the air and lit on an orange honeysuckle blossom.

"Drat that little scamp!" she said crossly, dropping the swatter to the porch. She scrunched up her face, and her large, round eyes became slits just like Miz Moonlight's.

"You still frettin' about moving out of state 'cause of your mama's job?" Grandma Talley asked, swiping again at the fly and missing.

"Yes, ma'am. California's so far away. Going to a new school, making new friends—it's scary. I can't imagine not sitting here with you, listening to your stories."

"I know, Kincaid, but things work out, most times better than we expect. You've got a lotta memories to take with you. Just remember to keep 'em tucked inside your heart."

"I wish I could stay with you forever," I said, tears brimming in my eyes. I turned away to stare at a doodlebug digging in the dirt so Grandma Talley wouldn't see.

"Don't you worry. You'll make new friends just fine."

She was right about one thing. I've got a lotta memories. Like climbing up the old chinaberry tree in our backyard. Baking teacakes and gingerbread in Grandma Talley's old wood stove. Sitting on the railroad tracks over Woman Hollering Creek with my best friend Bennie Jewel, fishing with bamboo poles. I'll cherish those memories forever.

I watched Grandma Talley squinting at the sun, making the large crow's feet lining her face resemble a patchwork quilt. I loved her wrinkles. I'll remember every crease line and fold in her face, for each one told of her life's story.

A huge collie the color of peanut brittle appeared from the Johnson house next door, yipping and yapping, trying to jump over the picket fence into the yard. Miz Moonlight sprang from my arms and streaked up the trunk of Grandma Talley's magnolia tree, fragrant with giant pearl blossoms.

"Scat, get away from here now, causing trouble," Grandma Talley scolded the dog.

He trotted off down the street, his tail between his legs, haunches low.

"Come on, let's go inside. Got somethin' to show you." Grandma Talley rose from the chair, holding onto her straw hat with one hand and picking up her wood cane with the other. I followed her through the screen door, stopping for a moment to place the dirty glasses in the kitchen sink, the pitcher of tea in the icebox.

She limped toward the hall closet, her cane tapping along the floor, me close on her heels. She opened the closet door and placed her straw hat on the top shelf. She patted down her spit-curled hair that had been mussed by her hat and began searching through stacks of clutter on the closet floor.

---

1. Use this space to define any unfamiliar words you circled. You can use context clues to guess at the meaning, but use a dictionary to confirm the correct definition.

Word	Definition
gossamer	

2. Which of the following best describes how Kincaid is feeling?

   a. Sad about moving to California

   b. Excited to go away

   c. Frustrated with her grandma

   d. Scared of the collie

3. In Activity 17, you learned that stories have a beginning, middle, and end. The conflict, or problem, is usually introduced in the beginning or middle. Reread Part 2 of "My Grandma Talley," and search for clues that help you figure out what the problem is. What seems to be the conflict of the story so far? What clues helped you find this conflict?

___

4. Reread paragraph 9. How do you think Kincaid feels in this paragraph? Explain how you drew this inference.

___

Analyzing Conflict 65

Activity 21: Writing about Conflict

1. In Part 2 of "My Grandma Talley," the reader finally figures out the conflict that Kincaid is facing. How is the conflict similar to the conflict in "The Gift"? How is it different?

   _____
   _____
   _____
   _____
   _____
   _____
   _____
   _____

2. How was the conflict in "The Gift" resolved?

   _____
   _____
   _____
   _____
   _____
   _____
   _____

3. How do you predict the conflict in "My Grandma Talley" will be solved?

   _____
   _____
   _____
   _____
   _____
   _____
   _____

4. What conflict will your story include? How will your characters feel about it?

　

5. How will the conflict in your story be resolved? Remember that in some stories, the problem is fully solved and everyone lives happily ever after. But sometimes, the characters learn a life lesson instead. You don't need to have the problem fully solved, but you do have to give the reader a sense of closure, or an end to the story.

Writing about Conflict

6. Now take the main character in your story, and imagine the thoughts that are running through their head as they face the main conflict in the story. Do a freewrite as your character, imagining what sorts of things they would say to themselves.

Activity 22: Conflict Resolution

>> **Read Part 3 of the story below.**

My Grandma Talley (Part 3)

by Nadine Oduor

"Grandmama never wrote much down, except for birthdays and deaths noted in the old family Bible. No, Grandmama told her stories and gave me this." Grandma Talley smiled warmly, dragging out an old trunk. "A trunk full of precious memories."

Inside the trunk were old clothes, a glittering jewelry box, family pictures, a huge black Bible, handwritten letters scrawled on paper frayed and yellowed with age, and an ancient quilt.

I sifted through the pictures and spotted one of a young woman in a 1920s teal flapper's dress, white leggings, button-down shoes, and a spit-curl hairstyle.

"That's you!" I squealed with delight.

"Yes, still wet behind the ears," Grandma Talley chuckled.

"You look beautiful!" I gushed.

"Why, thank you. I think so too, I must say." She grinned, opening the jewelry box.

She held up a pair of rose-colored earrings with a matching necklace of rainbow crystal hearts.

"These were given to me by Aunt Elnora for my sixteenth birthday," she said. "I've held on to 'em long enough. Here, you take them. They're your going-away gift." She placed the jewelry into my hand, and her laughter floated through the house sweet as the taste of jelly beans.

I clipped the earrings to my ears and draped the necklace around my neck. My eyes surely sparkled as bright as my rose-colored earrings. "Thank you," I mumbled. I wasn't wearing royal robes, only a T-shirt and flowered shorts, but I felt like a beautiful African princess!

Grandma Talley gazed admiringly at me. "Our family's made up of our ancestors—grandfathers, grandmothers, my mother, father, sisters and brothers. You have some of them inside you. Memories are a patchwork quilt of our lives, Kincaid, and it's up to us to choose which patches we stitch into it. I've taught you the way my grandmama taught me, like her grandmother before her, passing on our stories to those coming after us."

Grandma Talley carefully lifted out a quilt and laid it on her bed. I sat on one of the oak chairs next to her.

"When we tell our stories, we pass them on to the next generation and honor those who came before us. Grandmama gave this to me when I was just about your age," she said, unfolding the quilt.

She held up the quilt that seemed old as time itself. "This was taken from my wedding dress when I married your Grandpa Wilford," she said touching a patch of satin the color of ecru.

"This is from the dress in your photo," I said, pointing out a teal patch.

"Yes. And one day you'll give this quilt to your daughter, who'll pass it on to her daughter. Remember, Kincaid, we take our loved ones in our hearts wherever we go. I won't be more than a heartbeat away." She smiled, hugging me tightly.

Miz Moonlight meowed loudly at the front door till I let her inside. I picked her up, and she nestled contentedly in the crook of my arm. I pulled the ancient quilt around me under the silver blue Texas moon and leaned my head against Grandma Talley's soft shoulder.

In my heart I knew I'd make new memories, but I'd keep the treasure of precious old ones wrapped up deep inside me, the heritage of a wonderful family.

1. Reread paragraph 10. Which of these options best explains why Kincaid feels beautiful?

    a. She is wearing expensive jewelry.

    b. She is wearing royal robes.

    c. She feels connected to her family.

    d. She has just styled her hair.

2. Reread paragraph 9. Then reread this sentence from Part 1: "Grandma Talley's deep molasses laugh made her stomach jiggle, and I imagined her laughter bubbling up inside her heart to her throat, then sashaying out her caramel-colored lips." What words related to taste do you notice in these descriptions? Why do you think the author chose to use these words?

3. The quilt in this story is used as a symbol for how a family fits together. What things make up the quilt that Grandma Talley shows Kincaid? Why do you think she chose to use these things to add to the quilt?

___

4. In Part 2 of "My Grandma Talley," we learned that Kincaid is nervous about moving to California. How is this conflict resolved in Part 3?

___

Activity 23: Bringing It Home

1. How does the author resolve the conflict in "My Grandma Talley"? Did you correctly predict the ending in Activity 21? Are all of the problems solved? If not, how does the reader get a sense of closure?

   _____
   _____
   _____
   _____
   _____
   _____
   _____
   _____

2. How does Kincaid change over the course of "My Grandma Talley"? Choose text evidence to support your answer.

   _____
   _____
   _____
   _____
   _____
   _____
   _____

3. Grandama Talley tells Kincaid, "Memories are a patchwork quilt of our lives, Kincaid, and it's up to us to choose which patches we stitch into it." What are some pieces that make up the quilt of your life? What memories do you treasure? Choose at least three, and describe them.

4. Grandma Talley has a trunk of precious memories that help her remember her family and her childhood. Use this space to write a letter to your future self. What do you want your future self to remember about this age? Is there any advice you'd like to give yourself? Any questions you want to ask?

Activity 24: Diving into Fantasy

>> Read Part 1 of the story below. As you read, circle unfamiliar words.

Save a Kingdom (Part 1)

by Maggie Murphy

Prince Gethyn stared at the curving, green-gray stone wall's ornately carved door. He'd never felt so nervous. Pushing back his long fair hair, he reminded himself to stand tall.

Rose watched over this mysterious place, going in and out often. Gethyn couldn't recall ever seeing her without its door's heavy key dangling from her waist-sash. This enchanted key, decorated with a gold-tailed crystal comet, set its own rules, seldom opening the door for others. Today would be the first time Gethyn saw the Oval's hidden world of merfolk, talking animals, fairies. But, he thought, mine's no holiday outing.

"Cheer up, Gethyn," said Clew, Rose's sparrow-sized scarlet dragon.

Clinging to the sorceress's ivory cloak, he looked like a fantastical enameled brooch come to life. "You'll do fine, just as your father did."

Gethyn's answer was out before he could stop himself. "But Clew, I couldn't be more different than Father!"

Clew waved a glittering ruby claw. "Folks aren't meant to be alike. What's the worry in that?"

Gethyn gave an inward sigh, thinking, The problem is this: I'm not strong and bold, and oh, what will happen if I don't . . . ?

Of course, he already knew. In Gethyn's small island kingdom of Wystivere, firstborn princes and princesses couldn't count on ascending to the throne. Instead, they confirmed their eventual right to rule by passing a royal test given at fifteen years of age. Once Rose's key revealed Gethyn's task, he'd enter the Oval and have four hours to meet his goal. As an only child, if he failed, the next chance at the crown went to a distant relative, a duke. This young man spent nearly all his time at his castle on the mainland, showing scant interest in the quiet, mist-wrapped isle Gethyn cherished.

Rose placed the key on Gethyn's palm. Across its comet's tail, silver words engraved themselves. He read, "To rule Wystivere, Prince Gethyn must save a kingdom."

Gethyn almost dropped the key. "Save a kingdom? Rose, I . . ."

"It does sound daunting," said Rose, her gray eyes thoughtful. "I myself have no foreknowledge of the key's challenges, but remember: they are not mock situations contrived for the tests. Somewhere in the Oval, an entire kingdom needs you now, just as all of Wystivere will one day if you're crowned king. Trust the quest-magic to turn your footsteps in the right direction; trust in yourself enough to try your best." Gently, she touched Gethyn's shoulder. "Begin, Gethyn, and Godspeed."

Clew winked an amber eye. "From me, a dragon blessing: May you glide, not flap."

"Thank you, friends," said Gethyn, managing a weak smile before turning the key in the lock. The moment the door opened, the key's comet blazed with a crimson light that would fade as Gethyn's allotted time ran out. He threaded his belt through the key's handle and stepped inside.

Within the Oval, enchanted acres stretched unconfined by the wall's measurements. Gethyn gazed at flower-spangled meadows, lush willows, rushing streams. A firebird flew by, its feathers a radiant mosaic of apricot, white, and saffron. The slender spires of a city rose in the distance, gleaming like silver reeds.

I can't see any other city, thought Gethyn. That has to be the kingdom that's in danger. Worrying about what the trouble is—don't think of manticores!—won't help me get there faster.

Gethyn hiked for hours, but the city remained distressingly far off.

Around noon, he caught a flash of red in the sky. It's Clew, he thought, keeping an eye on me. It lifts my spirits to see him, but how I wish he had better progress to report.

1. Use this space to define any unfamiliar words you circled. You can use context clues to guess at the meaning, but use a dictionary to confirm the correct definition.

Word	Definition
manticore	

> There are many *genres*, or types, of fiction. The last two stories you read are examples of realistic fiction. A story that is realistic fiction is made-up but takes place in the real world and seems like it could be true. For example, "My Grandma Talley" is not a true story, but it is common for people to move and miss their family. This make it feel real. "Save a Kingdom" is fantasy. That means it takes place in a world that is different from ours and may include magic and/or magical creatures like dragons.
>
> Other common fictional genres include science fiction, mystery, and historical fiction. Science fiction stories take place in a world that is slightly different than ours but has a scientific explanation. Mysteries have a mystery that has to be solved by the end of the story. And historical fiction is fiction that is set in the past.

2. Reread Part 1, and put a star next to the details that tell about the world this story takes place. List three details below.

   _____

   _____

   _____

3. This story begins with action, and the reader has to figure out what is happening in the beginning of the story. What is Gethyn's task in this story?

   a. To fight the kingdom of Wystivere and win

   b. To enter the Oval and complete an assignment so that he can become king

   c. To help Rose and Clew get into the Oval so they can go home

   d. To defeat the duke who is trying to take over his kingdom

4. Reread paragraphs 4–6. Does Gethyn feel confident in himself in these paragraphs? What do we learn about the way he sees himself?

   _____

   _____

   _____

   _____

Diving into Fantasy

Activity 25: Building Character

1. In Part 1 of this story, we have already learned a lot about Gethyn. Now it's time to read like a writer. Pay attention to the things Maggie Murphy does in this story that help us get to know Gethyn. List at least two actions, thoughts, and things that Gethyn says.

Actions	Thoughts	Words

2. Now write a short analysis: How does Maggie Murphy show us Gethyn's personality in Part 1 of "Save a Kingdom"? Be sure to include evidence from the text to support your response.

___

3. Now look back at the three characters from your own story that you wrote about in Activity 19. Fill out the chart for them. Think about how you can show their personality through their actions, thoughts, and words.

Character Name	Actions	Thoughts	Words

4. How does Gethyn feel about his father? How can you tell?

_____
_____
_____
_____
_____
_____
_____
_____
_____
_____

Building Character

5. How will your characters feel about each other? Are they alike or different? Do they get along, or do they argue?

Activity 26: Understanding Character

>> Read Part 2 below. Circle any unfamiliar words.

Save a Kingdom (Part 2)
by Maggie Murphy

Not long after, Gethyn crossed a stone bridge spanning a gorge. To his left, looped around a sturdy oak at the cliff's edge, a frayed rope with a few planks knotted to it streamed out like a kite's tail in the high wind.

So here's where the old bridge used to be, thought Gethyn. I don't know how Father had the courage to take a single step onto it.

For that had been King Edric's test. When Gethyn was a child, Clew had told him the tale of his father's bravery. "The key sent your father," Clew had said, "to rescue a certain not-too-powerful fairy who'd unwisely stored most of the magic she did have in her fancy new gold wand.

"Back then, the one bridge over the ravine near this fairy's cottage was an abandoned, half-ruined web of ropes and boards. She had no wings, our fairy, but she wasn't concerned about falling. She'd blithely stroll across this flimsy sky-way, relying on her wand's enchantments to prevent missteps. But then came the heart-stopping morning when, at the bridge's center, she dropped her wand into the gorge. Too horrified to move, she clutched the moldy rope railing for dear life, shrieking for help. Your father picked his way out to her, led her to safety, and climbed down into the ravine to fetch her wand. He left the Oval hours early and ate his oatcake—simply to honor the day!—back at your castle."

I'm not even close to my fairy city yet, Gethyn thought anxiously, toiling up a tall hill near the bridge. On its far side, he descended into wildly overgrown terrain that proved almost impassable. Gethyn pushed ahead, with branches catching at his cloak, thorns piercing his tunic, and thick mud gripping his boots.

Finally the dense vegetation gave way to a windswept, eerie landscape of black rock formations, everything from graceful arches to rows of lumpy, twisted pillars that reminded Gethyn of weird trollish faces.

The city lay not far beyond, but Gethyn soon found that wending his way through the strangely shaped rocks was like negotiating a maze.

Again and again, dead ends forced him to double back. For the fifth time, he checked the key; its glow had dimmed alarmingly. He then looked up to a terrifying sight. On a nearby peak, a purple dragon that dwarfed the tall pines around it uncoiled its sinuous body, spread its wings, and dived straight toward the fairies' realm.

Gethyn fought the urge to hide, thinking, No! I have to sound the alarm! He yelled out warnings, but with the wind whipping his screams away, he might as well have been a mewling kitten. The dragon swept low, wheeled, spit a column of flame into the city, and sped off. Smoke plumed upward. Gethyn heard the fairies shouting.

He scrambled over piles of boulders, skirted pits, and raced along winding, rock-ribbed passageways. Then he came to yet another craggy barrier, but this wall had a large, low hole in its center. Gethyn dropped to his knees and saw that it led to a clear route out of the rocks.

At that instant, tiny voices cried, "Hear our plea!" and an ebony ribbon of ants poured from a crevice. Gethyn wanted to groan. But despite the awful timing of this new delay, he couldn't bring himself to ignore the piteous little creatures.

One ant stepped forward. "A heavy rain has washed away our food stores," it said. "Have you anything to spare?"

"My oatcake, gladly." Gethyn opened his bag, carefully placed the cake beside the ants, and crawled through the gap as they chorused their thanks. Minutes later, he was leaping and skidding down a steep, pebbly slope to the city's high, white-marble wall.

1. Use this space to define any unfamiliar words you circled. You can use context clues to guess at the meaning, but use a dictionary to confirm the correct definition.

Word	Definition
gorge	

2. Reread this sentence: "Finally the dense vegetation gave way to a windswept, eerie landscape of black rock formations, everything from graceful arches to rows of lumpy, twisted pillars that reminded Gethyn of weird <u>trollish</u> faces." Think about why the author chose to use the word *trollish*. What effect does it have on the sentence?

   a. It makes the landscape feel cute, like a doll.

   b. It makes the place sound creepy, and it makes Gethyn nervous.

   c. It makes it seem like everything in the place is secretly alive.

   d. It makes the pillars seem cheerful and neat, like in a happy space.

3. Reread paragraphs 3 and 4. How would you describe Gethyn's father? What evidence supports your description?

   _____
   _____
   _____
   _____

4. Why did Gethyn stop to help the ants? What evidence supports this?

   _____
   _____
   _____
   _____

5. Compare and contrast Gethyn and his father. Use text evidence to support your answer.

   _____
   _____
   _____
   _____
   _____
   _____
   _____
   _____

Understanding Character

Activity 27

Dialogue

Dialogue is an important part of a story. The things that characters say to one another can help demonstrate their personality, as we say in Activity 25. They can also help to explain things to the reader or move the plot along. Look at these sentences again:

One ant stepped forward. "A heavy rain has washed away our food stores," *it said.* "Have you anything to spare?"

Notice that quotes surround all of the words said by the ant. The first word inside the quotes (*A* and *Have*) are capitalized because they start a new sentence. At the end of the first sentence of dialogue (*A heavy rain has washed away our food stores*), there is a comma inside the quotation mark. That is because it is followed by the words *it said*, and the period comes at the end of the full sentence. The second sentence ends with a question mark that is inside the quotation mark.

1. The following sentences all have punctuation errors. Correct the errors, and write the sentence correctly.

   - "I wish I could come." I told my sister.

   _____

   _____

   _____

   - My sister explained, "You don't have a bathing suit, so you can't go swimming,"

   _____

   _____

   _____

   - "I promise I'll just play in the sand." I pleaded.

   _____

   _____

   _____

84 Kumon English Language Arts Reading & Writing

2. Reread paragraphs 3 and 4 from Part 2 of "Save a Kingdom." Why do you think the author chose to include this piece of dialogue? What does the reader learn?

3. Reread the dialogue between Gethyn and the ants. How would you describe the way the ants speak to him? How does he speak to them? Why is that important to the story?

4. Brainstorm some things your characters might say that relates to the conflict in your story. Record them below. Be sure to punctuate them correctly.

Character	Dialogue

Activity 28: Plotting It Out

>> Read Part 3. Circle any unfamiliar words.

Save a Kingdom (Part 3)

by Maggie Murphy

Once he arrived, Gethyn couldn't spot a single fairy on the battlements or in the airy windows of the elegant, gold-veined towers. He ran what seemed an endless way searching for a door, only to discover the one he finally found shut fast. Frantically, he hammered on it until a crescent-shaped window hidden in one of its silvery panels swung open, revealing a gray-bearded gatekeeper.

"Please let me in to help carry water!" begged Gethyn. "The fire—"

"Is under control," the gatekeeper said.

"Is anyone hurt?"

"No, no. But I can't tarry now, nor allow you inside, on our queen's strictest orders." And the window snapped shut.

Why shouldn't the fairy queen lock me out? Gethyn thought miserably. I journeyed here too slowly to do her people any good. But how grateful I am that no one was harmed; it's what truly matters to me. I'll remind myself of that every time I regret today. A tear slipped down his scratched, dusty face as the crystal comet's faint light flickered out and its message smoothed itself flat like writing lost on wave-washed sand.

Turning, Gethyn saw that with his test over, the Oval's wall stood just yards away. These easy steps back felt more difficult than his trek. Instead of saving a kingdom, he thought, I've lost the kingdom I love.

Still, if I can't be like Father in most ways, I can be like him in some: I won't complain or make excuses. Gethyn marched through the doorway and met Rose's gaze squarely.

But before he could speak, she said, "Well done, Gethyn. I'm delighted to congratulate you on winning the crown!"

"I've already soared up to the castle to tell your father and mother," Clew said eagerly. "The rule barring them from waiting here is terribly hard on parents. I left them cheery as court jesters!"

It's even worse than I expected, thought Gethyn, glancing at Clew's merry face. Somehow, poor Clew has misheard the news from the magical city. "Rose, Clew," he said firmly, "I'm sorry to disappoint you, but there's been a mistake. I was too far away for my warnings about the dragon to do any good, and the fairies themselves put out the fire."

Clew grinned. "No they didn't. And if you had doused those flames, it's you who'd have needed rescuing! You reached the fairy city just in time to view a grand old tradition. The dragon you thought tried to set the place ablaze merely dropped in to light the fairies' feast-day bonfire."

"That banquet is the reason the fairy queen had you so abruptly turned away," Rose said. "An ordinary person who partakes of the fairy folks' tempting enchanted food or drink must remain with them forever."

"I see," said Gethyn. "But what I don't understand is how I could possibly have succeeded in my quest."

"Clew has carried someone here who takes great pleasure in sharing that story." From the folds of her cloak, Rose drew out a firebird feather, its cool white light spilling through her fingers. Gethyn felt more bewildered than ever until, at the feather's center, he spied a black speck: an ant.

"Now do you understand, Gethyn?" asked Rose softly.

Gethyn nodded, a quiet joy filling his heart.

The ant called out, its familiar piping voice sure and clear, "Gethyn refused to leave the humble to their fate! His oatcake has provided bountiful food for our desperate nation. I hereby proudly proclaim that today Prince Gethyn of Wystivere did indeed save a kingdom!"

1. Use this space to define any unfamiliar words you circled. You can use context clues to guess at the meaning, but use a dictionary to confirm the correct definition.

Word	Definition
battlements	

2. In just three sentences, write a short summary that tells how Gethyn was able to complete his challenge and save a kingdom.

___

3. What is a possible theme for this story?

___

4. This story takes place in a fictional world. Could the theme you identified also make sense in our world? Why or why not?

___

5. How does Gethryn change from the beginning of the story to the end? Use text evidence to support your answer.

___

Plotting It Out 89

Activity 29 — Organizing Events

1. Now that you have finished reading "Save a Kingdom," use this chart to organize the events that happen in the story. Some events have been added for you.

Beginning	Rose gives Gethyn the key to the Oval.
Middle	Gethyn sees a fire. Gethyn is stopped by a colony of ants.
End	

2. How do these events unfold to create an engaging story?

_____
_____
_____
_____

3. Now it's time to begin outlining your own story. Use this chart to plan out the events that will take place in your story. What is important to introduce in the beginning? When will you introduce the conflict? How will the characters respond? How will you resolve the conflict in the end?

Beginning	
Middle	
End	

Organizing Events

4. Now use the remaining space to begin drafting your story. You can start at the beginning of the story if you wish, but you can also choose an event in the middle to start drafting first. Remember: this is not the final draft. You can make changes to it before you finish the story.

Activity 30: Reading Biography

>> Read the biography below. Circle any unfamiliar words.

Pathways into the Library
by Aileen Easterbrook

From the time he was a young boy, James Haskins always had a book in his hand. While other kids were outside playing ball, Jim was usually reading. He could be found in one of his favorite places: curled up underneath the kitchen table or up in the tree that grew in his front yard.

Jim was born in Demopolis, Alabama, during the time of segregation. Because Jim was Black, he was not allowed to check out a single book at the public library. Libraries were for whites only. The laws of segregation separated Jim from all the books he longed to read.

But Jim read everything he could get his eyes on. He read all two hundred books in his school library. He read cereal boxes, signs, and license plates. He read an entire set of encyclopedias from A to Z. Jim convinced a teacher at school to lend him books of her own. He even managed to get some public library books through a white woman whom his mom worked for doing laundry.

When Jim was a teenager, Black Americans' struggle for equal rights was becoming the civil rights movement. Many brave people were taking risks by refusing to follow unfair segregation laws. Jim went to Montgomery, Alabama, and joined a civil rights group. The group was headed by Dr. Martin Luther King, Jr. Jim believed in King's nonviolent approach to change. Once, during a peaceful march, Jim was arrested. Because of that, his college expelled him.

Jim did graduate from college. Afterward, he went on to teach school in Harlem, a part of New York City. As a teacher, he had trouble finding books that interested his Black students. So he decided to write his own books about successful Black Americans. Through his writing, he met and interviewed many of the people he admired, including Rosa Parks.

Today, libraries have more than one hundred books written by Jim Haskins, the boy who loved to read, and today, children of all races can walk through the doors of any public library and find interesting books that inform, entertain, and inspire them.

1. Use this space to define any unfamiliar words you circled. You can use context clues to guess at the meaning, but use a dictionary to confirm the correct definition.

Word	Definition
segregation	

> Biographies tell the true story of a person's life. They may not follow the same plot structure as a story, but they do show a series of events that happen over time. And usually, in a biography, the person will face challenges, which can be similar to the conflict in a story.

2. What challenge did James Haskin face as a child?

_____

_____

_____

3. Reread paragraph 3. How would you describe Jim based on his actions in this paragraph? Why?

_____

_____

_____

4. Reread paragraph 5. How are Jim's actions in this paragraph similar to or different from his actions in paragraph 3? You can use these sentence structures: In paragraph 5, we learn that Jim _____. This is similar to/different from the way he _____ as a child because _____.

_____

_____

_____

_____

_____

Kumon English Language Arts Reading & Writing

5. In Activity 16, you read "The Gift," a short story about a boy who wants to buy a gift for his sister but doesn't have enough money. In "Pathways into the Library," you read about a real person, James Haskins, who wasn't able to borrow the books he wanted as a child due to segregation. In both texts, the main character wants something that is difficult for them to get. How are these characters and their lives alike? How are they different?

Activity 31: Using Signal Words

"Pathways into the Library" uses cause/effect signal words in several places. These are words that signal to the reader that there is a relationship between two ideas in the sentence: a cause and an effect.

Read the following examples:

1. "<u>Because</u> Jim was Black, he was not allowed to check out a single book at the public library."

   - The word *because* tells the reader that they are about to read the cause. The final part of the sentence contains the effect. So Jim couldn't borrow a book from the library because he was Black.

2. "Once, during a peaceful march, Jim was arrested. <u>Because of that</u>, his college expelled him."

   - The phrase *because of that* works similarly to the word *because*. The part that comes after this phrase tells the effect. So Jim's arrest caused him to be expelled from college.

3. "As a teacher, he had trouble finding books that interested his Black students. <u>So</u> he decided to write his own books about successful Black Americans."

   - The word *so* is followed by an effect. In this case, the fact that he couldn't find books for his students is the cause. The effect is that he wrote his own.

1. Rewrite the following sentences using a cause/effect signal word.

   a. I lost my backpack. I had to get new notebooks for school.

   _____

   _____

   b. I don't like spicy food. My mom waits to add hot peppers to a dish until after I take some.

   _____

   _____

c. I am not a very fast runner. My little brother can beat me in a race.

2. Look back at the draft you started in Activity 29. Choose two sentences that you can add cause/effect signal words to. Write them below.

   1. _____

   2. _____

Transition words and phrases are another set of words that can be very helpful for narrative writing. Transition words can help show the sequence of events or a change of setting. Some common words and phrases include *after, before, and then, during, immediately, later, while, soon, this time, above, beyond, nearby,* and *far from.*

3. Look back at "Save a Kingdom" and "Pathways into a Library." Find as many transition words and phrases as you can. List at least four examples here.

   1. _____

   2. _____

   3. _____

   4. _____

4. Now look back at your draft again. Find three places where you can add a transition word or phrase. Write the new sentences below.

   1. _____

   2. _____

   3. _____

Activity 32: Final Narrative Piece

>> **In this activity, you will write your polished narrative. Use the pieces you have already drafted to create your final story.**

Be sure to include:

- An introduction
- A conflict
- Resolution
- Characters
- Detailed events in a logical order

_____
_____
_____
_____
_____
_____
_____
_____
_____
_____
_____
_____
_____
_____
_____
_____
_____
_____
_____
_____

Kumon English Language Arts
Reading & Writing

ARGUMENT WRITING INTRO
Table of Contents

Activity	Title	Page
33:	A Persuasive Interview	104
34:	Brainstorming an Opinion	107
35:	Understanding Call to Action	110
36:	Understanding Tone	113
37:	Summarizing an Opinion Piece	116
38:	Reasons and Evidence	119
39:	Supporting a Claim	122
40:	Organizing and Drafting	125
41:	Analyzing a Conclusion	128
42:	Evaluating an Argument	131
43:	Analyzing an Opinion Piece	134
44:	Final Opinion Piece	137

We are all full of opinions—and who doesn't love to share their thoughts with others? A well-crafted opinion piece is a piece of writing that allows an author to share their views with the world. An opinion piece can take any form, including a speech, an op-ed, a letter, or a passionately written essay! In this section, you will read four opinion pieces and analyze them closely to see how each author builds their argument. Along the way, you will begin crafting your own essay using the strategies you see in each piece. Finally, you'll put it all together into a piece that lets you make your voice heard!

Activity 33: A Persuasive Interview

>> Read the interview below. Circle any unfamiliar words.

Fast-Tracking High-Speed Rail
by Kathiann M. Kowalski

High-speed trains zoom at speeds between 186 and 225 miles per hour (mph) in Japan, China, France, and elsewhere. Not so in the United States. Some trains in the Northeast can reach 150 mph. But most American trains go no faster than 80 mph.

The US High Speed Rail Association (USHSR) wants a national high-speed rail network by 2030, with new trains, modern signaling equipment, and 17,000 miles of new high-speed track. Built in phases, it would result in fast, efficient, and comfortable travel for people. USHSR's president Andy Kunz explains.

Why should the United States build high-speed rail?

High-speed rail is one single investment we can do that will help solve the climate crisis and the energy crisis at the same time. A third reason is just to have a fast and new high-capacity transportation system that actually gets people to their destination quickly and efficiently. Our highway delay congestion, combined with aviation delays, costs the nation about $140 billion per year in wasted time and fuel.

How would high-speed rail help with climate change?

The big thing about rail is it all can be powered by renewable energy. However, we need to be investing in and expanding our renewable energy a lot more than we are now—the same way we need to be investing in and expanding our rail system.

What's wrong with oil as a fuel?

It's extremely expensive. It's highly polluting.

Why would high-speed rail need new tracks?

To get to 200 mph speeds, you need to build separate, dedicated tracks. When you have freight trains carrying explosive chemicals on a track, it's not safe for a passenger train to be going 200 mph on the same track.

Wouldn't high-speed rail be expensive?

We're still spending approximately $200 billion a year as a nation expanding our road system, even when it's been quite obvious that driving has peaked. [It's time to] start readjusting how we invest in the transportation that we need to carry us forward in the 21st century.

A planned high-speed rail line between Los Angeles and San Francisco might not open until 2029. Why so long? Sometimes it takes longer to get permits and environmental clearances than it does to build the system. One of our goals is to streamline the process.

Why doesn't the United States have high-speed rail yet?

The big companies in energy and road-building and aviation are all in great fear of high-speed rail ever taking hold in America. When it does, their sales are going to drop a lot because commuters and travelers will have another choice for traveling long distances. These industries have been using their influence on Congress and state governors . . . to prevent high-speed rail from getting off the ground in America.

How do your group's plans for high-speed rail compare with the effort to build the transcontinental railroad 150 years ago?

If we could build the transcontinental railroad in six years then, we should definitely be able to build this whole rail system in 15 years today.

1. Use this space to define any unfamiliar words you circled. You can use context clues to guess at the meaning, but use a dictionary to confirm the correct definition.

Word	Definition
congestion	

A Persuasive Interview 105

2. This opinion piece is structured as an interview. We are learning Andy Kunz's opinion, and the author, Kathiann M. Kowalski, is asking questions to guide his argument. Which of the following opinions do you think Andy Kulz would most likely agree with?

   a. The US needs to build better airports.

   b. More Americans should drive so that trains aren't as crowded.

   c. The US should build more high-speed rail.

   d. Train tracks take too long to build, so we should use cars.

3. Which of the following is NOT a reason to build high-speed rail?

   a. Airplanes are often delayed.

   b. Trains can be run on renewable energy.

   c. Cars get stuck in traffic.

   d. New tracks are expensive to build.

4. There are seven questions in this interview. Which one allows Andy Kulz to state his main opinion the most clearly? What does he say his opinion is?

   _____
   _____
   _____
   _____
   _____

5. Why do you think Kathiann M. Kowalski asks, "Wouldn't high-speed rail be expensive?" How does Andy Kulz answer her?

   _____
   _____
   _____
   _____
   _____

Activity 34: Brainstorming an Opinion

1. Are you persusaded by Andy Kulz's argument? Why or why not? Write a short letter to him in response telling him your opinion.

2. In Activity 44, you will write your own opinion piece. You will have many activities to develop your thoughts. In this activity you will choose your topic and your claim. You can choose from the following prompts or a topic of your own. Write the topic you choose in the space below.

   - Should kids be able to vote?
   - How long should weekends be?
   - Should people be required to compost?
   - Should all kids be required to play a sport?

   _____
   _____
   _____

3. Use this space to do a freewrite about the topic you chose. Don't worry about writing something polished. Just write down your thoughts without editing them. You can use this freewrite to help figure out what your opinion is about the topic.

4. Now it's time to draft your claim. Read your freewrite, and think about how you can state your opinion clearly. You should be able to write the answer in one sentence. You don't need to give a reason yet.

_____
_____
_____
_____
_____
_____

5. Imagine that someone interviews you about your topic. What questions might they ask you? Brainstorm at least five questions.

_____
_____
_____
_____
_____
_____
_____
_____
_____
_____
_____

Activity 35: Understanding Call to Action

>> Read the opinion piece below. Circle any unfamiliar words.

Children Who Shaped History

Not all history has been made by grown-ups. Young people also have performed daring deeds and contributed to America's development with their acts of determination and compassion. Some of these children were geniuses or incredibly talented, while others were resolved only to do or be the best they could.

During the Revolution, sixteen-year-old Sybil Ludington rode horseback through the night to warn militia members of the approaching British. From that war through the Civil War, teenage boys volunteered and served as drummers, sometimes at the cost of their lives. Auguste Chouteau was only fourteen when his stepfather put him in charge of a group of men who sailed up the Mississippi River to build the trading post that became the city of St. Louis. And Sacajawea was just two years older than that when, with a newborn baby, she accepted the responsibility of helping to guide Lewis and Clark through the Northwest. In the early twentieth century, when times were hard for families in the Northeast, children went to work to help their families. Workers in the mines and textile mills often were only ten or twelve years old or even younger.

Two noteworthy children became famous because of a single act of determination to fix something that bothered them. Samantha Smith wrote a letter to the premier of the Soviet Union, challenging him with her fears about nuclear war. Grace Bedell had Abraham Lincoln's future in mind when she wrote to him, but her letter changed the way we remember this great man.

A special talent has brought many young people fame and admiration. At four years old, Hilda Conkling started "talking poetry," and her first book of poems was published when she was ten. Shirley Temple's bright eyes, sweet smile, and energetic acting abilities were known throughout the world by the time she was seven. Children such as Tracy Austin, Cassius Clay, and Bobby Jones have excelled in sports, and Bobby Fischer was a chess champion at age twelve.

Each generation has included some special children who helped shape their times. We would like to know what young people of this generation might do to contribute to history. Remember: an action does not have to be spectacular to make a difference in the world.

1. Use this space to define any unfamiliar words you circled. You can use context clues to guess at the meaning, but use a dictionary to confirm the correct definition.

Word	Definition
resolved	

2. What is the main opinion, or claim? How can you tell?

___
___
___
___
___

3. This piece contains many examples that help to prove the claim. List three examples below.

___
___
___
___
___

> Some opinion pieces end with what is called a "call to action." This is when the author prompts the audience to do something to help the problem they have identified.

Understanding Call to Action 111

4. *Each generation has included some special children who helped shape their times. We would like to know what young people of this generation might do to contribute to history. Remember: an action does not have to be spectacular to make a difference in the world.* Why do you think this piece ended with this paragraph? What was the author hoping to accomplish? How did it make you feel when you read it?

Activity 36: Understanding Tone

1. Reread this quote from "Children Who Shaped History":

   "Young people also have performed daring deeds and contributed to America's development with their acts of determination and compassion. Some of these children were geniuses or incredibly talented, while others were resolved only to do or be the best they could."

   How would you describe the tone, or feeling, of this quote?

2. What words help to create this feeling? Why?

3. Opinion pieces can have many different tones. Some are funny, while others are outraged and passionate. Some are meant to inspire, and some are written in a clear, educational manner. The tone should match the subject matter. What would an appropriate tone be for the topic you have chosen? Why?

_____
_____
_____
_____
_____
_____
_____

4. How can you include a call to action in your opinion piece? Practice writing one here.

_____
_____
_____
_____
_____
_____
_____
_____
_____
_____

5. Reread this paragraph again: "Each generation has included some special children who helped shape their times. We would like to know what young people of this generation might do to contribute to history. Remember: an action does not have to be spectacular to make a difference in the world." What is an issue in our modern society that you think we should be working on? How could a kid contribute to this action?

Activity 37: Summarizing an Opinion Piece

>> Read the text below, and circle any unfamiliar words.

Back to the Tap (Part 1)

by Jodie Mangor

Voss comes from Norway. Bisleri is bottled in India. Évian is a French brand. Fiji comes from, well, Fiji. In the United States alone, there are more than 80 brands of bottled water. In 2019, Americans drank more than 14.4 billion gallons of bottled water. That makes the United States one of the top bottled-water-consuming nations. In the last decade, growing numbers of people have been making the switch to bottled water from sugary, caffeinated soft drinks. That seems to be a healthy choice, right? Yet, while it may be healthy for humans, is it a wise one for the planet?

Water for One

A single-serve water bottle offers great convenience. It's light. It doesn't go bad. It doesn't need to be refrigerated to be consumed. It can be bought almost anywhere. It can be carried around for a while before being thrown away.

Convenience isn't the only reason for bottled water's rise in popularity. Adjectives such as *pure* and *pristine* are used to describe the product. Words such as *rejuvenating* and *healthy hydration* are used to sell it. Images of beautiful mountains or massive natural glaciers accompany marketing ads. Many people believe that bottled water is cleaner and more healthful than tap water from public water systems.

Tap Water Truths

That is a misconception. In developed nations such as the United States and in Europe, regulations ensure safe tap water. In fact, rules often are stricter for tap water than they are for bottled water. In the United States, tap water is regulated by the U.S. Environmental Protection Agency (EPA). By federal law, tap water is supposed to be tested every year to make sure it is safe to drink. Bottled water is not held to that same testing standard. Viewed as a packaged food product, bottled water is regulated by the U.S. Food and Drug Administration (FDA). And state governments are in charge of regulating bottled water that is packaged and sold within their borders.

Individual states don't have the same regulations. Tap water also often contains naturally present minerals, such as calcium and magnesium. Another mineral, fluoride, often is added. Those minerals make tap water healthful.

Did you know that as much as 40 percent of the water bottled in the United States starts out as tap water? Before bottling, some companies filter it. They also might add minerals for taste. Yet, despite its sometimes-humble origins, bottled water can cost up to 10,000 times more per gallon than tap water. And for every bottle of water, three times that amount of water is needed to produce it.

1. Use this space to define any unfamiliar words you circled. You can use context clues to guess at the meaning, but use a dictionary to confirm the correct definition.

Word	Definition
pristine	

2. Use the chart below to summarize the main points in each paragraph.

Paragraph 1	
Paragraph 2	
Paragraph 3	
Paragraph 4	
Paragraph 5	
Paragraph 6	

Summarizing an Opinion Piece

3. Based on the summary you wrote, what do you think the opinion, or claim, of this piece is? How can you tell? Keep in mind that the author may not state the claim directly.

   _____
   _____
   _____
   _____
   _____

4. Based on what you just read, which is healthier to drink: bottled water or tap water? Use evidence from the text to support your answer.

   _____
   _____
   _____
   _____
   _____

5. Reread paragraph 3. Why do you think companies use these words to describe the water they sell?

   _____
   _____
   _____
   _____
   _____

Activity 38

Reasons and Evidence

> The author of an opinion text uses reasons and evidence to support their claim. A reason is a point that the author makes about why their claim is true. The evidence is a specific fact or example that proves it.
>
> For example, imagine that you are reading an opinion text about why everyone should wear school uniforms. A reason might be that since everyone is wearing the same clothing, no one will feel left out or bullied for wearing clothes that aren't cool. A piece of evidence might be something like, "In a study, researchers found that students are 20% less likely to be bullied if they attend a school where uniforms are required."

1. The section "Water for One" is about why bottled water is popular. What are two reasons the author presents for why bottled water is so popular? What evidence does she use to support these reasons?

Reason	Evidence
Many people believe that bottled water is cleaner and more healthful than tap water.	

2. The section "Tap Water Truths" is about why bottled water isn't necessarily better than tap water. What reasons and evidence does the author use to support this point?

Reason	Evidence

3. Now think about your own opinion piece. Draft three reasons to support your claim.

_____
_____
_____
_____
_____
_____

4. Now find the evidence to support your claim. You may already know an example or fact to support your reason, but you may need to do some research. Have an adult help you find at least one piece of evidence to support each reason. List them here.

_____
_____
_____
_____
_____
_____
_____
_____

Activity 39: Supporting a Claim

>> Read the text below, and circle any unfamiliar words.

Back to the Tap (Part 2)
by Jodie Mangor

Environmental Impact

The impact of bottled water on the environment is staggering. Approximately 2.7 million tons of plastic are turned into disposable bottles each year. The manufacturing of all those bottles requires large quantities of crude oil and water. That process produces greenhouse gases. Bottled water is often shipped long distances to reach consumers, sometimes across vast continents. The transportation of the product uses even more fossil fuels and creates more pollution. And although plastic bottles can be recycled, only a fraction of them are. The United States recycles only about 25 percent. The rest of the bottles are part of a growing solid waste problem.

Is Bottled Ever Better?

At times, bottled water is the best available option. Hurricanes, other natural disasters, and emergency situations can make public water unsafe to drink. Reliable water systems may not be in place in developing nations and war-torn countries. In those cases, bottled water can provide an important source of clean and safe drinking water.

The residents of Flint, Michigan, know this firsthand. In 2014, Flint officials were looking to save money. They decided to switch to the Flint River as the source of the city's water supply. The water from the river was not treated. As it traveled through the city's old pipes, it carried dangerously high levels of lead into people's homes. Unknowing residents, including children, became sick after drinking their newly sourced tap water. Flint's residents spent several years trying to get the city to take responsibility for their lead-filled water. Finally, in 2017, an agreement was reached. The city was told to remove the old pipes and water lines and replace them with safe new water lines by 2020. Until safe tap water was available, the city had to provide its citizens with safe bottled drinking water.

1. Use this space to define any unfamiliar words you circled. You can use context clues to guess at the meaning, but use a dictionary to confirm the correct definition.

Word	Definition
crude oil	

2. Reread paragraph 1. How does this paragraph help to defend the author's claim? Use text evidence to support your answer.

_____
_____
_____
_____
_____
_____
_____
_____
_____
_____
_____
_____
_____
_____
_____

> In an opinion piece, authors use reasons and evidence to prove their claims. But sometimes, they will acknowledge certain exceptions to their claim. This can make the argument stronger, since it shows that the author is considering the issue thoroughly.

Supporting a Claim

3. Now reread paragraphs 2 and 3. Does this section support the author's claim? Why do you think this section was included?

___

4. What effect do the section titles have? Why do you think the author chose to organize the piece this way?

___

Activity 40: Organizing and Drafting

1. "Back to the Tap" is divided into sections with headings. These headings organize the essay into different parts. You can use the same approach in your own piece if you choose, or you can simply organize it by having each body paragraph focus on one reason with evidence to support it. Use the sample structure below to create your outline.

Paragraph 1: Introduction	
Paragraph 2: Reason 1	
Paragraph 2: Evidence for Reason 1	
Paragraph 3: Reason 2	
Paragraph 3: Evidence for Reason 2	
Paragraph 4: Reason 3	
Paragraph 4: Evidence for Reason 3	
Paragraph 5: Conclusion	

2. Use the remaining space here to begin drafting your body paragraphs.

Activity 41: Analyzing a Conclusion

>> Read the text below, and circle any unfamiliar words.

Back to the Tap (Part 3)
by Jodie Mangor

Future Solutions

"Back to the tap" movements are cropping up around the world. They encourage people to use tap water and reusable "sports" bottles rather than bottled water. Doing so can save money, use fewer resources, and create less waste. Colleges and universities have begun to ban the use and sale of bottled water on their campuses. San Francisco, Concord (Massachusetts), and other cities across the United States have adopted bans on single-serve water bottles. Places in Canada (Toronto), Australia (New South Wales), and several states in India have taken similar action.

Many bottled water companies are trying to do their part. They have reduced the amount of plastic in their bottles and bottle caps. Both the Colorado-based BIOTA company and the British company Belu use biodegradable plastic bottles derived from a renewable source: corn. Belu takes it a step further by donating its net profits to WaterAid. WaterAid is a charity that works to bring clean water to people who don't have access to it. Bottled water has become an international phenomenon, and it can be an important source of safe drinking water. We should not lose sight of a more environmentally friendly source, however: the water that comes out of our taps.

1. Use this space to define any unfamiliar words you circled. You can use context clues to guess at the meaning, but use a dictionary to confirm the correct definition.

Word	Definition
net profits	

2. What is the "back to the tap" movement?

_____

_____

_____

3. Which of the following things are bottled water companies NOT doing to help the environment?

   a. Using biodegradable materials

   b. Reducing the amount of plastic in their caps

   c. Banning plastic water bottles in cities

   d. Donating to charities

4. Do you think the author believes that bottled water companies are doing enough to help the environment? Support your answer with text evidence.

_____

_____

_____

_____

_____

_____

_____

_____

5. Has the author persuaded you? Why or why not?

Activity 42: Evaluating an Argument

1. What positive things did you learn about bottled water in this piece? What negative things did you learn about bottled water?

   _____
   _____
   _____
   _____
   _____
   _____
   _____
   _____

2. How did the author build her argument throughout all three sections? What did you think of the way she organized her ideas? Was it clear or confusing? Did she provide sufficient reasons and evidence to support her claim?

   _____
   _____
   _____
   _____
   _____
   _____
   _____
   _____
   _____
   _____

3. Reread the last two sentences of the text: *Bottled water has become an international phenomenon, and it can be an important source of safe drinking water. We should not lose sight of a more environmentally friendly source, however: the water that comes out of our taps.*

   Why do you think the author chose to acknowledge the importance of bottled water while also advising that we use less of it? Does this help or hurt her argument? Why?

   _____
   _____
   _____
   _____
   _____
   _____
   _____
   _____

4. Can your argument be strengthened by acknowledging why someone might disagree with you? Use this space to imagine what someone who disagreed with you might say about your argument.

   _____
   _____
   _____
   _____
   _____
   _____
   _____
   _____

5. Write a letter to a friend expressing your opinion about bottled water. Do you agree that it is harmful to the environment? Do you think it is important to have in some situations? Why or why not? Make sure to respond to respond to the points made in "Back to the Tap."

Activity 43: Analyzing an Opinion Piece

Read the text below, and circle any unfamiliar words.

What's in a (Dog's) Name?
by Lee Gjertsen Malone

"What kind of dog is that?" It's a question every mixed-breed dog owner gets. And many are happy to answer, whether it's to say, "Pomeranian-schnauzer-rottweiler" or "bulldog-Lab" or even just their best guess. Research out of Arizona State University (ASU) a few years ago, though, shows humans are really bad at guessing the breed makeup of our beloved mutts. What's more, doing so may actually hurt some shelter dogs' chances to get adopted.

"Shelter dogs are a lot more interesting and unique than we've ever given them credit for," says Lisa Gunter. She's a professor of animal sciences at Virginia Tech and conducted this research while a doctoral student at ASU. Along with Clive Wynne, she has studied dog breed labeling from different angles. Their research shows that rushing to label mixed-breed dogs, especially non-purebred dogs, may not be a good idea.

In one study, the researchers tested the DNA of nearly 1,000 shelter dogs to learn more about their breed or breeds. Among some of that group, staff had correctly identified the breeds of just one in 10 dogs.

Even for those labeled correctly, Gunter says, the relationship between a dog's breed and its overall demeanor and behavior is not always clear. And for mixed-breed dogs, it's often not at all what people expect. "It's not like mixing paint colors," she says. "Even when we do know the breeds of the dog, we don't know how it's going to work out for that individual dog."

The biggest negatives arise for dogs labeled as breeds that many people mistrust, like pit bulls. The same scientists examined that mistrust in another study, showing videos of similar-looking dogs to shelter visitors. But they labeled some as pit-bull-type breeds and others as another breed, such as Labrador retriever. The researchers found that participants' opinions of the same dog changed if they thought it was a pit-bull-type breed.

In 2014, one shelter, Orange County Animal Services in Florida, decided to remove breed information from its kennels entirely. The ASU researchers found that the shelter's adoption rates increased by more than 70 percent for dogs that would have been labeled as pit bulls. In fact, adoption rates for all groups of dogs improved. And the length of time dogs waited for adoption went down.

"We bring along a lot of baggage about what a dog is supposed to be because of what we've heard about the breed," Gunter says. But "dogs are complex. When we remove labels, the dogs can be whatever the people want them to be."

1. Use this space to define any unfamiliar words you circled. You can use context clues to guess at the meaning, but use a dictionary to confirm the correct definition.

Word	Definition
demeanor	

2. What is the author's claim? Restate it in your own words and explain how you determined it was the claim.

___
___
___
___
___
___
___

Analyzing an Opinion Piece

3. Use this chart to organize the reasons and evidence presented in this piece.

Reason	Example or Evidence That Supports the Reason
Labeling mix-breed dogs is difficult.	In one study, only 1 in 10 shelter dogs were correctly identified by breed.

4. Describe how the author uses reasons and evidence to support the claim. Are you persuaded by this argument?

_____
_____
_____
_____
_____
_____
_____

Activity 44: Final Opinion Piece

>> **In this activity, you will write your polished opinion piece. Use the work you have already drafted to create your final piece.**

Be sure to include:

- A clear claim
- An introduction that hooks the reader
- Reasons to support the claim
- Facts, or evidence
- A conclusion that ties it all together

_____
_____
_____
_____
_____
_____
_____
_____
_____
_____
_____
_____
_____
_____
_____
_____
_____
_____

Answer Key

Many answers will vary. Sample answers for some questions are provided below. See our website for additional samples: https://kumonbooks.com/for-parents-educators/educators-guides.

Activity 1
2. The central idea of this text is that in ancient China, books were made by hand and were very expensive.
3. b
4. c
5. d

Activity 2
1. a. X They are including far too many details!
   b. X A summary should not contain your opinion.
   c. ✓

Activity 3
1. To find out the temperature from a long time ago, scientists search for proxies like coral, tree rings, and ice.
2. *Clues called "proxies"*
3. *water/plentiful/grew, drought/shrank*. Drought is when water is not plentiful.
5. *not just one*. A multitude means more than one.

Activity 4
3. The writer is talking directly to the reader. When I was reading the introduction, it helped me imagine that I was a scientist and needed to figure out the climate from long ago.
4. Gardiner starts off by describing how we figure out the temperature today—by looking at a thermometer. This is a familiar experience. But then she asks how we would find out the temperature from hundreds of years ago.

Activity 5
4. These headings help the reader understand how this long informational text is structured. This helps keep the information organized. Without the headings, the reader might be a little confused about how each part fits together.

Activity 7
3. b

Activity 9
2. c
3. Confucius's father died when he was young, and he was very close to his mother. He and his mother were very poor after his father died, and he was determined to honor his mother.
4. Confucius was too poor to have a tutor, but he attended a local school and studied on his own.

Activity 13
3. b

Activity 16
1. c
2. b
5. d

Activity 18
1. Grandma Talley, Kincaid, Miz Grissom, Miz Moonlight
2. On a hot, muggy day in Wink, Texas, on Grandma Talley's front porch.

Activity 20
2. a

Activity 22
1. c
2. *molasses, caramel*. Kincaid loves her grandmother, so she uses words that are sweet to describe her.

Activity 24
3. b

Activity 26
2. b

Activity 27
1. "I wish I could come," I told my sister.
   My sister explained, "You don't have a bathing suit, so you can't go swimming."
   "I promise I'll just play in the sand," I pleaded.

Activity 28
3. Treat everyone well, even if you don't think you will gain anything from it.

Activity 31
1. I lost my backpack, so I had to get new notebooks for school.
   Because I don't like spicy food, my mom waits to add hot peppers to a dish until after I take some.
   Since I'm not a very fast runner, my little brother can beat me in a race.

Activity 33

2. c
3. d
4. "Why should the United States build high-speed rail?"
   High-speed rail is one single investment we can do that will help solve the climate crisis and the energy crisis at the same time. A third reason is just to have a fast and new high-capacity transportation system that actually gets people to their destination quickly and efficiently.

Activity 35

2. Young people can contribute to the world, too. The text tells about lots of young people who have done impressive things that changed the course of history.

Activity 41

3. c